WORKBOOK FOR

FIGHT RIGHT

(A Guide to Julie Schwartz Gottman's Book)

We wish you the best of luck and hope that this book helps you achieve your goals.

NOW IS THE TIME TO CHECK OUT THE TOP TIPS FOR BEING SUCCESSFUL IN USING THIS BOOK.

➢ Realize before you go any further that lying to yourself is among the worst things you can do. While following this guide, be honest with yourself.

➢ Use this guidance with caution and thoroughness while you seek out a guardian. It must be an accountable individual.

➢ **Engrave the book's teachings and principles deeply into your mind. It needs to permeate your entire being.**

➢ **When you get to the notes section, really let your thoughts flow.**

➢ **It is not an illusion; everything is actually feasible here.**

BEGINNING THE PROCESS OF CHANGE

A STATE OF MIND THAT COULD TRANSFORM

While it might sound strange, fighting in love can actually be a good thing for your relationship.

<u>Practical Steps You Can Do Right Now</u>

Learning how to fairly and successfully fight can help you get to know each other better, stick to your limits, and work out problems that could hurt your relationship in the long run.

DIFFICULTY WITH PERPETUAL

THOUGHT

Even if you've listened
to your partner's
deepest, darkest secrets
and put up with their
most interesting smells
in bed in the mornings,
you and your partner are
still two different
people.

Everything that is been occupying your thoughts

This means that you live and experience life in different ways, and your different ways of understanding of events may not always match up.

In some cases, these differences can cause fights in the relationship. Even though it's never fun to spend time you could be cuddling working out a fight, these fights can sometimes be a big part of making your relationship stronger.

A fight is almost certain to happen at some point in a relationship. This is what happens when you live with someone or spend a lot of time with them.

FINAL ARTICLE!

There is good news: being angry with your partner is normal and healthy1–as long as you do it the right way.

A STATE OF MIND THAT COULD TRANSFORM

When you start to get angry because of something your partner did or said, take a deep breath and step back.

<u>Practical Steps You Can Do Right Now</u>

Here are some things you can do instead to have a quiet fight with your partner.

DIFFICULTY WITH PERPETUAL

THOUGHT

Even though fights
usually make people
angry, it's important to
keep your cool and say
calm things to your
partner when you
disagree.

Everything that is been occupying your thoughts

At the end of the day, every argument ought to revolve around the importance of good communication.

This means giving up the sharp, hurtful response you were planning. When you're fighting with your partner, it also means using nice words instead of harsh ones like "idiot," "fool," or "stupid."

An argument can quickly get worse if you use the wrong words. This can make things worse between you and your partner.

FINAL ARTICLE!

When you speak slowly and carefully during a fight, you can be more deliberate about getting your point across.

A STATE OF MIND THAT COULD TRANSFORM

You may be hurt and angry because of something your partner did, but it's important to try to see things from a different point of view when you're arguing.

Practical Steps You Can Do Right Now

By seeing things from your partner's point of view, you not only give yourself a chance to see things from different points of view, but you also put your partner's emotional needs ahead of winning a fight.

DIFFICULTY WITH PERPETUAL

THOUGHT

When you have a
disagreement, it's best
to try to find a
peaceful, understanding
answer.

EVERYTHING THAT IS BEEN

OCCUPYING YOUR THOUGHTS

It can be bad for the relationship if everything you say is meant to hurt your partner's feelings or show that you're right.

Not only will it make
your partner less likely
to talk to you about
problems in the
relationship, but it
could also drive a gap
between you two, which is

not what you want if you
want to be together in
the future.

Instead, pay attention to
what your partner says
and ask questions to make
sure you understand
everything.

FINAL ARTICLE!

It might be easier for your partner to understand what you want to say if you use requests instead of complains.

A STATE OF MIND THAT COULD TRANSFORM

Say something like, "The
bedroom is getting messy—
would you mind clearing
up your things?" instead
of "Why don't you ever
clean up after yourself?"

Practical Steps You Can Do Right Now

It's better to talk to
your partner straight
instead of putting them
down. This will help keep

the relationship calm and respectful.

DIFFICULTY WITH PERPETUAL

THOUGHT

To talk about all your problems, you and your partner need to make time to do so. If someone is talking, don't stop them unless you need to ask a question. If you do, be polite and avoid being angry.

Everything that is been occupying your thoughts

Sometimes, it might not be possible to end a fight in one day, especially if tempers and

feelings keep getting
worse.

In these kinds of
circumstances, it is
possible that you will
need to agree upon a
certain time in order to
continue your

conversations in a
healthy manner.

The majority of the time,
arguing with your spouse
is done within reasonable
bounds that prevent
putting anybody down.
This is because fighting

may be beneficial to your relationship.

FINAL ARTICLE!

When two people in a relationship fight without a good reason, it can have long-lasting effects. Research has shown that fights in marriage can cause worry, sadness, and even eating problems.

This is Day 5 of Your Transformation

A STATE OF MIND THAT COULD TRANSFORM

Even worse, this can hurt parents' relationships with their kids and make it harder for brothers to get along when there are kids in the picture.

Practical Steps You Can Do Right Now

Similarly, fights that turn violent are a sign

of a relationship that is
very unhealthy.

DIFFICULTY WITH PERPETUAL

THOUGHT

If you want to stay healthy and stop getting worse or more violent treatment, you should always leave an abusive partner.

Everything that is been occupying your thoughts

If you and your partner often get into fights that involve the

nonviolent parts listed
above, it might help to
talk about how to change.

It may be beneficial to
engage a counselor to
lead conversations in
order to get reliable
outcomes.

Fights, when handled
well, may be a learning
experience for partners,
which can help enhance
the relationship between
all parties involved.

FINAL ARTICLE!

A fight is a simple way to tell if your partner is still interested in being with you for a long time. Being able to deal with things as they come is key to a trouble-free life.

DAY 6 OF EMBRACING CHANGE

A STATE OF MIND THAT COULD TRANSFORM

In order for a
relationship to work,
both people involved must
be ready to go through
the awkwardness of
arguments. It is
especially important for
partners to communicate
clearly and with
kindness.

Practical Steps You Can Do Right Now

That means both people in
the relationship have to
be ready to deal with the

awkwardness of fights. It is very important for partners to talk to each other in a kind and clear way.

DIFFICULTY WITH PERPETUAL THOUGHT

It's good to know that disagreements can be treated in an adult and friendly way without

putting the relationship
at risk, as long as both
people are working to
solve the problem.

Everything that is been
occupying your thoughts

This way, partners can
talk about their regrets
and unhappiness without
taking up time or making
the other person angry.
In the end, this can help

make the bond stronger
and increase its chances
of staying.

When you and your partner
talk about your problems
and ask each other
questions when you're not
sure, you both learn new
things about each other.

There is a possibility that it is communication strategies, such as their voice being lower when they are experiencing a great deal of pain.

FINAL ARTICLE!

For example, they might know that certain things, like touching before bed, are necessary for their happiness. Sometimes it's just finding out what they want and what they're afraid of in the relationship.

A STATE OF MIND THAT COULD TRANSFORM

If you keep an environment that encourages open communication, free from abuse, and good conversation in general, you can fight without worrying that it will hurt the relationship in the long run.

Practical Steps You Can Do Right Now

Your partner shouldn't have to guess what's wrong or what you want them to do. Tell them exactly what you need and

be clear about it. This
will help you avoid any
anger or confusion.

DIFFICULTY WITH PERPETUAL

THOUGHT

That being said, if you
think your partner is
trying to tell you
something, ask them if
they need anything.

Everything that is been occupying your thoughts

Saying something like, "Hey, can you pick up and vacuum the living room?" is a straight way to get your partner to do

something useful, like
clean up the living room.

Also, let people know if
something is making you
feel bad. You could say
something like, "I'm
really sad right now.
Could you please make me
some tea and sit with
me?"

Tell your partner how grateful you are every time they do something nice for you. Use every chance you get to tell each other how grateful you are. Making your bond stronger is an easy and

effective way to make
your friendship better.

FINAL ARTICLE!

For instance, thank your
spouse for cooking
supper. They should also
appreciate lunch and
kitchen cleanup.

WELL DONE!

IT GIVES US GREAT PLEASURE
TO KNOW THAT YOU HAVE

REACHED THE CONCLUSION OF
THIS MANUAL.

EMBRACE WHAT YOU HAVE
LEARNED AND DO NOT LET IT
SLIP YOUR MIND.

DONATING COPIES IS A GREAT
WAY TO SHOW THAT YOU CARE
BY ALLOWING OTHERS TO
IMPROVE THEIR LIFE AS WELL.

Made in United States
Troutdale, OR
10/30/2024

24291696R00030